WITHDRAWN

ROCKFORD PUBLIC LIBRARY

Rockford, Illinois

www.rockfordpubliclibrary.org

815-965-9511

MATH ADVENTURES

Zookeeper for a Day

by Wendy Clemson
and David Clemson

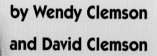

Math and curriculum
consultant: Debra Voege, M.A.,
science and math curriculum
resource teacher

GARETH**STEVENS**
GS
PUBLISHING
A Member of the WRC Media Family of Companies

Please visit our Web site at: www.garethstevens.com
For a free color catalog describing Gareth Stevens Publishing's
list of high-quality books and multimedia programs,
call 1-800-542-2595 (USA) or 1-800-387-3178 (Canada).
Gareth Stevens Publishing's fax: (414) 332-3567

Library of Congress Cataloging-in-Publication Data

Clemson, Wendy.
   Zookeeper for a day / Wendy Clemson and David Clemson. —
North American ed.
     p. cm. — (Math adventures)
   ISBN-13: 978-0-8368-7843-1 (lib. bdg.)
   ISBN-13: 978-0-8368-8142-4 (softcover)
   1. Arithmetic—Juvenile literature. 2. Zoo animals—
Juvenile literature. I. Clemson, David. II. Title.
  QA115.C546   2007
  513—dc22   2006052710

This North American edition first published in 2007 by
Gareth Stevens Publishing
A Member of the WRC Media Family of Companies
330 West Olive Street, Suite 100
Milwaukee, WI 53212 USA

This U.S. edition copyright © 2007 by Gareth Stevens, Inc. Original edition copyright © 2007 by ticktock
Entertainment Ltd. First published in Great Britain in 2006 by ticktock Media Ltd., Unit 2, Orchard Business Centre,
North Farm Road, Tunbridge Wells, Kent, TN2 3XF

ticktock project editor: Rebecca Clunes
ticktock project designer: Sara Greasley
Gareth Stevens editor: Tea Benduhn
Gareth Stevens art direction: Tammy West
Gareth Stevens graphic designer: Kami Strunsee
Gareth Stevens production: Jessica Yanke and Robert Kraus

Picture credits
t=top, b=bottom, l=left, r=right
Alamy/Jim West 23; CORBIS/Ariel Skelley 27; CORBIS/David Gray/Reuters 10-11; CORBIS/Reuters 8b; London Zoo 20;
Nature Photo Library/Lynn M. Stone 25tr; Science Photo Library/Alexis Rosenfeld 22; Shutterstock 1, 2, 4tl, 4br, 5,
6-7 (all), 9, 12-13 (all), 15, 16, 17, 18-19 (all), 21, 24, 25tl, 25b, 26 (all), 28-31 (all), 32; Ticktock Media Archive
4bl, 4tr, 8t, 15.

Printed in Canada

1 2 3 4 5 6 7 8 9 10 10 09 08 07 06

CONTENTS

MEASUREMENT CONVERSIONS

1 inch = 2.5 centimeters

1 foot = 0.3 meter

1 mile = 1.6 kilometers

1 pound = 0.5 kilogram

1 fluid ounce = 30 milliliters

WELCOME TO THE ZOO

Today, you will be helping the zookeepers at the City Zoo. Many of the animals at the zoo are endangered, which means there are not many of them left in the wild. Some animals are endangered because they have lost their habitats. Some animals are in danger because of hunters. The zoo, however, is a safe place for animals to live.

Taking care of zoo animals is an exciting and important job.

Zookeepers give the animals food and water.

Zookeepers and the zoo vet help the animals that are sick.

Zookeepers make the animals' enclosures interesting, with lots for the animals to do.

Visitors often ask the zookeepers questions about the animals.

Did you know that zookeepers need to use math?

Inside this book, you will find math puzzles that zookeepers have to solve every day. You will also have a chance to answer number questions about animals.

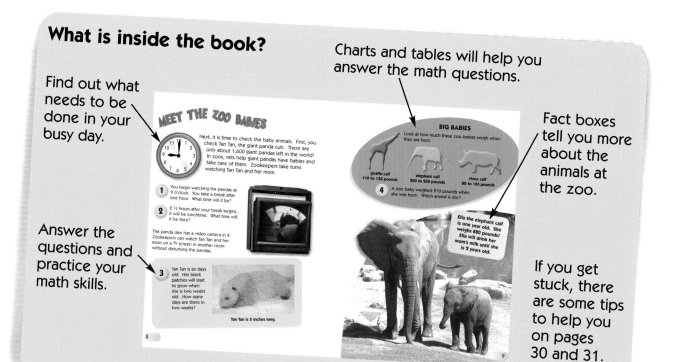

What is inside the book?

Find out what needs to be done in your busy day.

Charts and tables will help you answer the math questions.

Fact boxes tell you more about the animals at the zoo.

Answer the questions and practice your math skills.

If you get stuck, there are some tips to help you on pages 30 and 31.

Are you ready to be a zookeeper for the day?

You will need paper, a pencil, and a ruler, and don't forget to wear your rubber boots. Let's go!

TIME TO CHECK THE ANIMALS

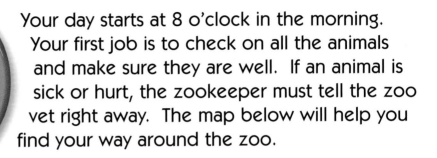

Your day starts at 8 o'clock in the morning. Your first job is to check on all the animals and make sure they are well. If an animal is sick or hurt, the zookeeper must tell the zoo vet right away. The map below will help you find your way around the zoo.

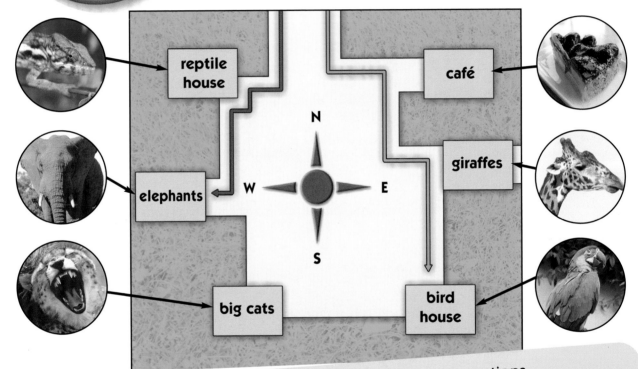

Use the zoo map above to answer these questions.

1 You walk past the café, the giraffes, the bird house, and the big cats. Are you walking clockwise or counterclockwise?

2 The giraffes are to the south of the café. What is directly to the west of the café?

3 How many right-angle turns do you make when you walk the length of the red path?

4 Now it is time to check the warthogs. Warty is waiting for his breakfast. Warty is 18 years old — that is very old for a warthog! What is the difference between your age and Warty's age?

In the wild, warthogs eat grass, berries, tree bark, and dead animals. In the zoo, they eat food pellets and vegetables.

WARTHOG TUSKS

Warthogs have four tusks. One of Warty's tusks is 8 inches long. Use a ruler to measure this line.

5 How much shorter is the line than Warty's tusk?

MEET THE ZOO BABIES

Now, it is time to check the baby animals. First, you check Tan Tan, the giant panda cub. There are only about 1,600 giant pandas left in the world! In zoos, vets help giant pandas have babies and take care of them. Zookeepers take turns watching Tan Tan and her mom.

The panda den has a video camera in it. Zookeepers can watch Tan Tan and her mom on a TV screen in another room without disturbing the pandas.

1 You begin watching the pandas at 9 o'clock. You take a break after one hour. What time is it now?

2 2½ hours after your break begins, it will be lunchtime. What time will it be then?

3 Tan Tan is six days old. Her black patches will start to grow when she is two weeks old. How many days are there in two weeks?

Tan Tan is 5 inches long.

BIG BABIES

Look at how much these zoo babies weigh when they are born.

giraffe calf
110 to 130 pounds

elephant calf
200 to 250 pounds

rhino calf
80 to 165 pounds

4 A zoo baby weighed 210 pounds when she was born. Which animal is she?

Ella, the elephant calf, is one year old. She weighs 880 pounds! Ella will drink her mom's milk until she is 2 years old.

KIMBA, THE BABY KANGAROO

Sometimes, animal moms become ill, and they cannot care for their babies. When a mom cannot feed her baby, the zookeepers have to feed the baby by hand. Kimba's mom is ill so the zookeepers have to feed Kimba. He needs four bottles of milk each day. It is your turn to give Kimba his bottle!

FEEDING KIMBA

Kimba drinks special kangaroo milk. To make the milk, you must add 2 spoonfuls of milk powder for every 1 fluid ounce of water.

1 How many spoonfuls of milk powder do you add to bottle A?

A

7 fluid ounces

2 How many spoonfuls do you add to bottle B?

B

11 fluid ounces

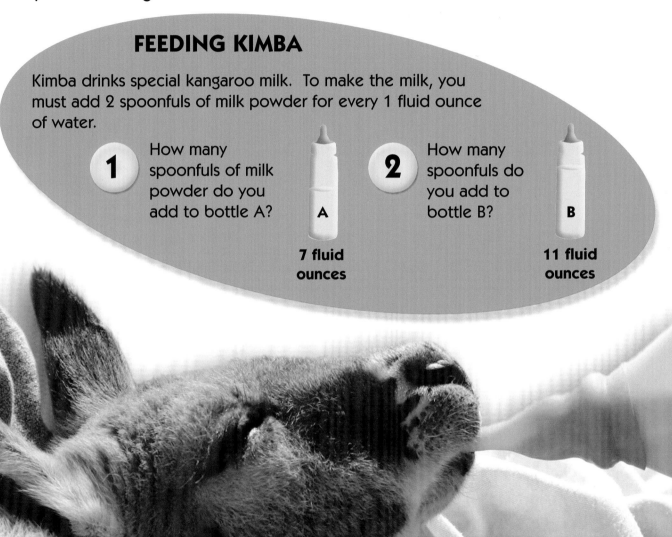

KIMBA'S WEIGHT

Zookeepers weigh animal babies regularly to make sure the babies are healthy and growing properly. Use the scale below each question to find the answer to the question.

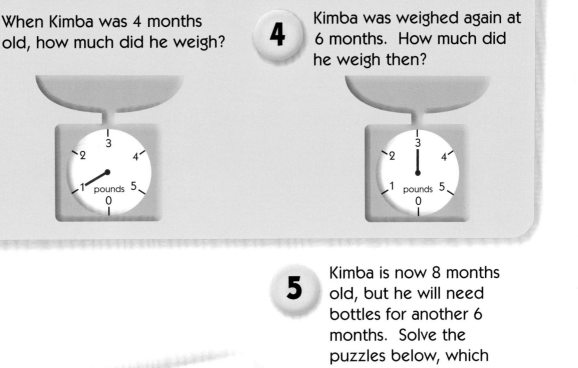

3 When Kimba was 4 months old, how much did he weigh?

4 Kimba was weighed again at 6 months. How much did he weigh then?

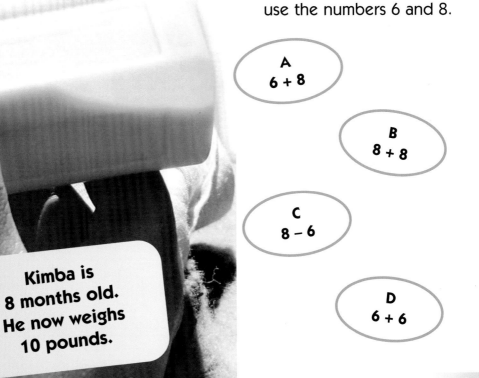

5 Kimba is now 8 months old, but he will need bottles for another 6 months. Solve the puzzles below, which use the numbers 6 and 8.

A
6 + 8

B
8 + 8

C
8 – 6

D
6 + 6

Kimba is 8 months old. He now weighs 10 pounds.

11

TODAY'S DELIVERY OF FOOD

The zoo animals eat fresh meat and vegetables. They also eat special pellets that give them the same vitamins as the food they would eat in the wild. A truck has just arrived. It is delivering carrots and mangoes. The pictures on the truck shows how many pounds of food the truck is carrying.

1 How many pounds of carrots is the truck to the right carrying?

2 If the delivery truck looked like the truck to the left, how many pounds of carrots would it be carrying?

3 There are 5 pounds of mangoes in a box. What is the total weight of 7 boxes of mangoes?

Chimpanzees love fruit!

FOOD CHART

Some animals eat only plants. They eat leaves, grass, fruits, or vegetables. Other animals are meat-eaters. They feed on insects, birds, fish, or mammals. Some animals eat plants and meat.

4 An animal name is missing from the bottom of the chart to the right. Which of the following three animals is the missing one?
- A tiger, which eats other animals
- An anteater, which eats insects and fruit
- A deer, which eats leaves and grass

animal names	plant eaters	meat eaters
otter		X
bear	X	X
hippo	X	
?	X	X

5 This zebra is given 1 bale of hay and ½ bucket of pellets at each meal. She is fed twice a day. How much does she eat each day?

LUNCH FOR THE ORANGUTANS

It is time to give the orangutans their lunch. They eat fruit. In the wild, orangutans live in rain forests. They spend all day looking for food. At the zoo, their food is spread around their cage. The zookeepers put the food in different places in the cage. Each day, the orangutans have to look for it, just like they would look for food in the wild.

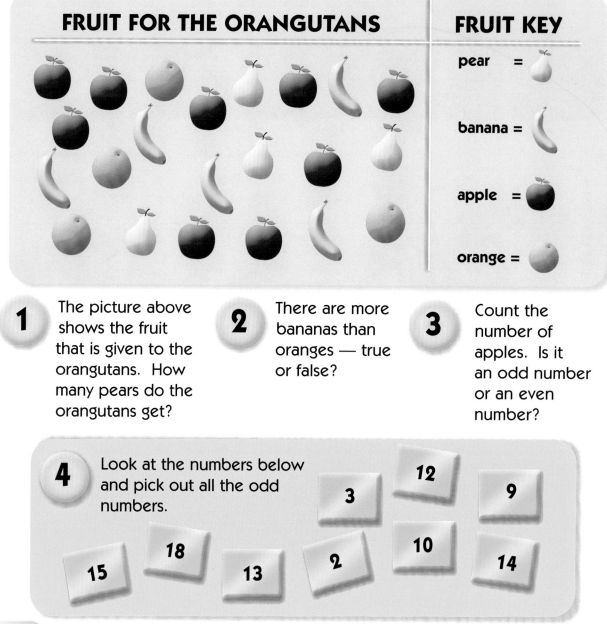

FRUIT FOR THE ORANGUTANS

FRUIT KEY

pear =

banana =

apple =

orange =

1 The picture above shows the fruit that is given to the orangutans. How many pears do the orangutans get?

2 There are more bananas than oranges — true or false?

3 Count the number of apples. Is it an odd number or an even number?

4 Look at the numbers below and pick out all the odd numbers.

12

3

9

18

10

15

13

2

14

5 Chang the orangutan is 24 months old.
How old is he in years?

6 Chang's friend, baby Bella, is 18 months old. How old is Bella in years?

Bella's mom is named Cindy. She is 23 years old.

SNAKES AND BIRDS

It is 2 o'clock. Time to help the zookeeper at the reptile house give a talk to the visitors. Visitors are allowed to touch the boa constrictor. Its skin feels dry and very smooth. The zookeeper says she feeds the snake rats and chicks.

THE ZOO'S LONGEST SNAKES

cobra   20 feet

python   30 feet   **rattlesnake**   8 feet

boa constrictor   15 feet

anaconda   26 feet

1 The boa constrictor is not the zoo's longest snake. Which snake is the longest?

2 Which snake is half the length of the python?

3 How many snakes are shorter than the cobra?

16

THE ZOO'S OLDEST BIRDS

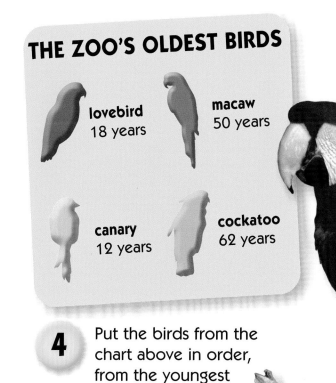

lovebird
18 years

macaw
50 years

canary
12 years

cockatoo
62 years

At the bird house, Mack the macaw says "hello" to the visitors. Macaws can copy words they hear. They practice until they get each word right.

4 Put the birds from the chart above in order, from the youngest bird to the oldest.

COUNTING THE BIRDS

The zookeepers have a chart to show how many birds are in the bird house.

types of birds	number in zoo
lovebirds	16
macaws	4
canaries	9
cockatoos	27

5 How many canaries does the zoo have?

6 What type of birds does the zoo have fewest of?

7 What type of birds does the zoo have the most of?

17

PLAYFUL PENGUINS

You check on the penguins next. The zoo has several types of penguins in one enclosure. The 8 Magellanic penguins are the newest. They arrived from a nearby zoo last week.

TYPES OF PENGUINS

Magellanic penguin

chinstrap penguin

king penguin

gentoo penguin

Penguins usually swim about 8 miles per hour, twice as fast as a fast human swimmer.

1 King penguins are 36 inches tall. Magellanic penguins are 9 inches shorter than king penguins. How tall are Magellanic penguins?

2 Chinstrap penguins are 6 inches shorter than king penguins. How tall are chinstrap penguins?

3 The smallest adult gentoo penguin is the same height as a chinstrap penguin. The largest is the same height as a king penguin. What is the range of heights gentoo penguins can be?

18

These are Magellanic penguins. In the wild, they live about 25 years, but in zoos, they can live as long as 30 years.

WHERE ARE THEY?

The zoo has 100 penguins. They can be found in the pool, on the rocks, or in their den.

 4 If there are 70 penguins on the rocks and 5 in the pool, how many are in the den?

 5 If there are 25 penguins in the pool and 20 in the den, how many are on the rocks?

CLEANING OUT THE GIRAFFE AREA

Oh, no! It is time to clean out the giraffes' enclosure. You sweep up the dirty straw and giraffe waste, or dung, and pile it into a wheelbarrow to take away. Then you spread out fresh, clean straw. That's better!

1 It takes 4 zookeepers 1 hour to clean the giraffe's enclosure. How long will it take 2 keepers?

Giraffes eat 75 pounds of food every day. In the zoo, they eat leaves, hay, and carrots.

A DUNG PICTOGRAM!

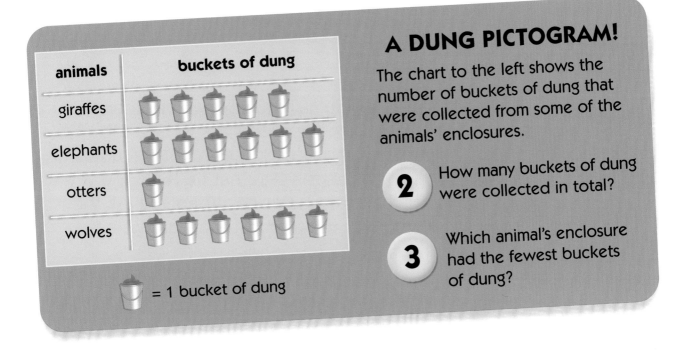

animals	buckets of dung
giraffes	🪣 🪣 🪣 🪣 🪣
elephants	🪣 🪣 🪣 🪣 🪣 🪣
otters	🪣
wolves	🪣 🪣 🪣 🪣 🪣 🪣

🪣 = 1 bucket of dung

The chart to the left shows the number of buckets of dung that were collected from some of the animals' enclosures.

2 How many buckets of dung were collected in total?

3 Which animal's enclosure had the fewest buckets of dung?

4 Straw comes in bundles called bales. How many bales are in each group below?

A   B   C

STRAW SHAPES

5 Some bales of straw have been pushed together. When you look at them you see the shapes to the right. How many sides does each of the shapes to the right have?

A

6 Can you name the shapes to the right?

B

21

STAYING HEALTHY

At 3 o'clock, you call the zoo vet because you are worried about one of the turtles. He is not diving underwater like the other turtles. You know this is a sign that he is ill. The vet gives the turtle medicine. Then you ask the vet to check the tiger cub because he has been limping.

TURTLE MEDICINE

A

B

C

The syringes above will help you answer the questions below. They contain different amounts of the turtle's medicine. The medicine is measured in milliliters (ml).

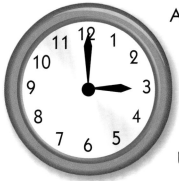

This turtle has not been eating. The vet is giving him medicine.

1 How many ml of medicine are in each of the syringes?

2 The turtle needs 10 ml of medicine. The vet uses two of the syringes. Which two does she use?

The vet checks the tiger cub's paws to see if any of them are hurt. A tiger's claws are retractable — they can be pulled inside the paws, just like a house cat's claws.

3 Tigers have 5 claws on each of their front paws and 4 claws on each of their back paws. How many claws do they have in total?

4 The tiger cub needs some vitamins. Each day, he is given 2 vitamin pills from the bottle below. How many days until the pills in the bottle are all used up?

20 vitamin pills

THE NIGHT HOUSE

Your next visit is to the Night House. This is where the nocturnal animals live. Nocturnal animals sleep during the day and wake up at night to look for food. The Night House is dark so the animals think it is nighttime. You step inside and wait for your eyes to get used to the dark.

In the zoo, fruit bats eat figs, oranges, pears, grapes, and watermelons.

BAT CHART

In the Night House, many of the bats are awake during the day. You count the bats that are awake at different times. The chart below shows your count.

1 How many bats were awake at 9:00 a.m.?

2 What time of day was it when the most bats were awake?

3 You think there should be at least 10 bats awake during the daytime. Has this happened?

time of day	numbers of bats awake
9:00 a.m.	32
noon	41
3:00 p.m.	27
midnight	2

4 Visitors like to know about the animals they see, so each enclosure lists information about the animals inside. Unfortunately, the labels have fallen off two of the enclosures in the Night House. Each animal's information sheet is missing two labels. You must decide which fact labels go with each animal. You know that:

• the tarsier's body is longer than the aye-aye's body.
• one of the animals has a tail that is twice as long as its body.

tarsier

• from Asia

aye-aye

• from Madagascar (Africa)

• body about 6 inches long

• body about 15 inches long

• tail about 20 inches long

• tail about 12 inches long

Like most nocturnal animals, this bush baby has big eyes to help it see in the dark.

THE PETTING ZOO

In the petting zoo, some of the tamer animals are kept in one big enclosure. Children can go into this fenced area and pet the animals. It is getting late, but there are still lots of visitors in the petting zoo. You warn the visitors that the zoo will be closing soon.

PETTING ZOO HUNDRED CHART

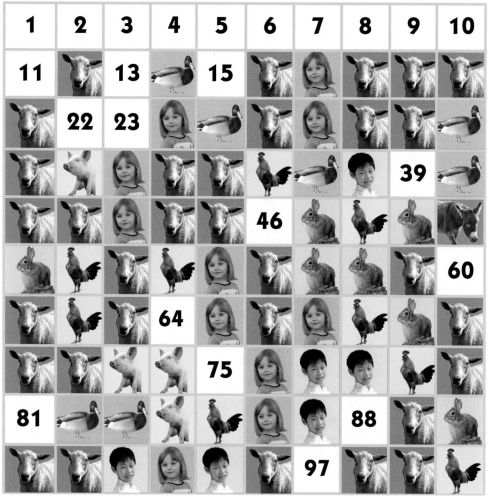

Look at the Hundred Chart above. It will help you answer the questions on the next page.

Sometimes, visitors are allowed to feed the animals in the petting zoo.

1. Animal **A** says, "I am on square 83. What animal am I?"

2. Animal **B** says, "I am on a square that is 3 tens and 2 ones. What animal am I?"

3. On which number square is there a donkey?

4. How many rabbits are there on the hundred chart?

5. How many squares have children in them?

THE ZOO SHOP

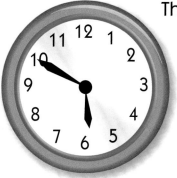

There are only 10 minutes left until the zoo closes. You have just enough time to go to the zoo shop to buy your friend a present. The shop is very important to the zoo. It raises money to help pay the zookeepers who take care of the animals.

1 The tiger posters cost $2.50 each. You have $5.00. How many posters can you buy?

2 If you had $10.00, how many posters could you buy?

JIGSAW OR BOOK?

JAGUAR JIGSAW 100 pieces!

$5 + 25¢ + 25¢ + 10¢ + 5¢

$5 + 25¢ + 10¢ + 5¢ + 5¢

3 How much does the jigsaw cost?

4 How much does the book cost?

HOW MUCH DO THE KEY RINGS COST?

A $3.60

B $2.50

C $1.70

D $1.50

5 Which key rings cost less than $2?

6 Which key rings cost less than $3?

7 What is the change from $5 if you buy key ring B?

Your day at the zoo is over. You need to rest, and so do the animals. It will be another busy day tomorrow.

TIPS AND HELP

PAGES 6-7

Clockwise - is the direction the hands of a clock move.

Counterclockwise - is the opposite direction.

clockwise   counterclockwise

Right angle - There are four right angles in a square. A right angle is often shown like this:

right angle

PAGES 8-9

Telling time - The shorter hand is the hour hand. It shows us what hour (or "o'clock") it is. The longer hand is the minute hand. It shows how many minutes until the hour or past the hour.

A week - There are seven days in one week.

PAGES 10-11

Twice as many - If there are two spoonfuls of powder in one fluid ounce of water, there are twice as many spoonfuls as fluid ounces. Double the fluid ounces to get the number of spoonfuls.

Scales - In math, scales help us see measurements. Check the scale to see what type of measurement is shown. For example, Kimba's scale measures pounds. The needle points to the number of pounds.

Adding - You can add numbers in any order. So the sum of 8 + 6 is the same as the sum of 6 + 8.

Subtracting (taking away) - It is important to put the bigger number first: 8 – 6 leaves the answer 2.

PAGES 12-13

Counting by tens - It is useful to be able to count by tens from 0 to 100. The pattern is: 0, 10, 20, 30, 40, 50, 60, 70, 80, 90, 100.

Chart - A chart is a good way to compare at least two kinds of information. The chart shows that the missing animal eats both plants and meat. Which animal eats plants such as fruit and meat such as insects?

PAGES 14-15

Odds and evens - Even numbers are in the pattern of counting by twos: 2, 4, 6, 8, 10, and so on. Odd numbers are the numbers that are not even: 1, 3, 5, 7, 9, and so on. Try counting by twos up to 20. Now count the odd numbers from 1 to 19.

A year - There are 12 months in a year. When you have a birthday, you become one year older.

PAGES 16-17

Putting numbers in order - The smallest whole numbers have no tens (only units, or ones). They are the numbers 1, 2, 3, 4, 5, 6, 7, 8, and 9. Next, look for numbers with only 1 ten, such as 12, and put the number with the fewest units first, then the others. Then see if there is a number with more than 1 ten.

PAGES 18-19

A range - A range starts at the smallest measurement and goes to the largest measurement.

Making 100 - To find a missing number, start by adding together the numbers you have, then take away that total from 100.

PAGES 20-21

Side - In math, a flat shape is said to have sides. To count the sides, start from one side and move around the shape, like this:

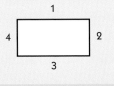

PAGES 22-23

Measurements - Use the syringes like scales. Check to see what type of measurement is shown. The syringes measure milliliters. The amount of liquid each syringe holds is marked by a line showing the number of milliliters.

Counting by twos - Count out loud: 2, 4, 6, 8, 10, 12, 14, 16, 18, 20. Each number means one day's amount of pills. How many times did you count a number of pills? That number of times is the number of days.

PAGES 24-25

Daytime - 9:00 a.m., noon, and 3:00 p.m. are all times during the day. Midnight is a time during the night.

Twice - means times two (x 2), so "twice as long" means "two times as long."

PAGES 26-27

Hundred Chart - This is a chart made of ten rows, each with ten numbers in it. The numbers go from left to right and from 1 to 100, counting from the first row downward. The chart is a good way to lay out one hundred numbers because you can use it to find number patterns.

PAGES 28-29

Dollars and cents - Two dollars and fifty cents can be written as $2.50. We use the "dot" between the 2 and the 5 to separate the dollars and the cents.

ANSWERS

PAGES 6-7

1 clockwise
2 reptile house
3 5 right-angle turns
4 If you are 5, the answer is 13.
  If you are 6, the answer is 12.
  If you are 7, the answer is 11.
  If you are 8, the answer is 10.
  If you are 9, the answer is 9.
  If you are 10, the answer is 8.
5 4 inches shorter

PAGES 8-9

1 10 o'clock
2 12:30 in the afternoon
3 14 days
4 elephant calf

PAGES 10-11

1 14 spoonfuls
2 22 spoonfuls
3 1 pound
4 3 pounds
5 A = 14
  B = 16
  C = 2
  D = 12

PAGES 12-13

1 80 pounds
2 160 pounds
3 35 pounds
4 anteater
5 2 bales of hay and
  1 bucket of pellets

PAGES 14-15

1 4 pears
2 true – 5 bananas
  and 4 oranges
3 9 apples – an
  odd number
4 3, 9, 13, and 15
5 2 years
6 1½ years

PAGES 16-17

1 python
2 boa constrictor
3 2 – the rattlesnake
  and the boa
  constrictor
4 canary, lovebird
  macaw, cockatoo
5 9
6 macaws
7 cockatoos

PAGES 18-19

1 27 inches tall
2 30 inches tall
3 30 to 36 inches tall
4 25 are in the den
5 55 are on the rocks

PAGES 20-21

1 2 hours
2 18 buckets
3 otters
4 A = 3 bales
  B = 5 bales
  C = 4 bales
5 A = 4 sides
  B = 4 sides
6 A = square
  B = rectangle

PAGES 22-23

1 A = 6 ml
  B = 2 ml
  C = 8 ml
2 B and C
3 18 claws
4 10 days

PAGES 24-25

1 32 bats
2 noon
3 yes
4 The tarsier's body is 15 inches long.
  The tarsier's tail is 20 inches long.
  The aye-aye's body is 6 inches long.
  The aye-aye's tail is 12 inches long.

PAGES 26-27

1 duck
2 pig
3 square 50
4 7 rabbits
5 17 squares have
  children in them.

PAGES 28-29

1 2 posters
2 4 posters
3 $5.65
4 $5.45
5 C and D
6 B, C, and D
7 $2.50